T0387054

FROSTING & ICING
WORKSHOP

Decorating Desserts

Megan Borgert-Spaniol

Abdo & Daughters
MIDDLE GRADE NONFICTION
An imprint of Abdo Publishing
abdobooks.com

ABDOBOOKS.COM

Published by Abdo Publishing, a division of ABDO, PO Box 398166, Minneapolis, Minnesota 55439. Copyright © 2024 by Abdo Consulting Group, Inc. International copyrights reserved in all countries. No part of this book may be reproduced in any form without written permission from the publisher. Abdo & Daughters™ is a trademark and logo of Abdo Publishing.

Printed in the United States of America, North Mankato, Minnesota
052023
092023

Design: Aruna Rangarajan and Emily O'Malley, Mighty Media, Inc.
Production: Mighty Media, Inc.
Editor: Ruthie Van Oosbree
Cover Photographs: Mighty Media, Inc.; Shutterstock Images
Recipes: Megan Borgert-Spaniol
Interior Photographs: iStockphoto, pp. 5 (bottom), 26; John Timbs/Wikimedia Commons, p. 7; Mighty Media, Inc., pp. 30 (cake), 32 (all), 36 (cake and bowl of sprinkles), 38 (all), 39 (all), 40–41, 42 (doughnuts), 44 (all), 45 (all), 46–47, 48 (cake and bowl of icing), 50 (all), 51 (all), 52–53; Shutterstock Images, pp. 3, 4, 5 (top), 6 (all), 8, 9, 10, 11 (all), 12 (all), 13 (all), 14, 15 (all), 16 (all), 17 (all), 18 (all), 19 (all), 20 (all), 21 (all), 22, 23 (all), 24, 25 (all), 27 (all), 28, 29 (all), 30 (background), 36 (background), 42 (background), 48 (background), 54 (background), 55, 56, 57, 58 (all), 59 (all), 60, 61 (all)
Design Elements: Shutterstock Images

Library of Congress Control Number: 2022948836

PUBLISHER'S CATALOGING-IN-PUBLICATION DATA

Names: Borgert-Spaniol, Megan, author.
Title: Frosting & icing workshop: decorating desserts / by Megan Borgert-Spaniol
Other title: decorating desserts
Description: Minneapolis, Minnesota : Abdo Publishing, 2024 | Series: Kitchen to career | Includes online resources and index.
Identifiers: ISBN 9781098291419 (lib. bdg.) | ISBN 9781098277871 (ebook)
Subjects: LCSH: Food--Juvenile literature. | Cooking--Juvenile literature. | Baking--Juvenile literature. | Icings (Confectionery)--Juvenile literature. | Cake icings--Juvenile literature. | Cookie icings--Juvenile literature. | Desserts--Juvenile literature. | Occupations--Juvenile literature.
Classification: DDC 641.865--dc23

CONTENTS

MAKING A CAREER IN THE KITCHEN

Are you fascinated by the way chocolate and cream form silky ganache icing? Do you love whipping sugar and butter into pillowy frosting? Can you see yourself piping intricate details onto cakes and cookies? If your answer to these questions is yes, you might be suited to a career as a baker or pastry artist.

Becoming a baker takes training and hard work. It takes dedication to service, quality, and safety. But if you have a passion for desserts, you may find that the dedication comes naturally and the hard work is worthwhile.

In this book, you'll learn about the history of decorated desserts and how they have changed over time. You'll become familiar with basic ingredients, tools, and techniques used to create frostings and icings. You'll practice using these ingredients, tools, and techniques in a few basic recipes. Then, you'll try your hand at following your own tastes and inspirations to modify recipes. Finally, you'll learn how you might turn your passion for desserts into a career.

Many bakers use royal icing to decorate cookies, gingerbread houses, and intricate wedding cakes. This is because royal icing is durable and has a smooth look.

Frosted cupcakes first appeared in the early 1900s, around the same time that buttercream frosting was invented.

Buttercream frosting is usually used as cake filling or as decoration for cakes or cupcakes. It can be flavored and dyed different colors.

FROSTINGS & ICINGS

Frostings and icings are sweet spreads used to coat or top cakes, cookies, and other desserts. These spreads serve various purposes. They add flavor, texture, and visual interest to desserts. They also create a protective layer that seals in moisture so the dessert doesn't dry out as quickly.

So, what's the difference between frosting and icing? You might see the words used interchangeably in cookbooks and online recipes. But many experts say the difference comes down to consistency. Frosting is thick, fluffy, and easy to spread over baked goods. Meanwhile, icing is thinner and shinier than frosting.

It's typically used to create a glossy coating or detailed decorations.

Desserts, especially cakes, have been embellished with frostings and icings for hundreds of years. Icing dates to at least the mid-1600s, when English recipe writer Rebecca Price instructed bakers to cover a cake with beaten egg whites and sugar. The smooth mixture of sugar and egg whites eventually earned the name "royal icing" after it was used to decorate the wedding cake of England's Queen Victoria in 1840.

Queen Victoria's cake started a trend toward multitiered wedding cakes covered in white icing. The refined white sugar used to make

Queen Victoria and Prince Albert's cake was created by John Mauditt, the Queen's confectioner. It featured Britannia, the female figure of Britain, and the bride and groom in Roman attire with the queen's favorite dog.

In the past, white wedding cakes indicated wealth since refined sugar was so expensive.

the icing was expensive at the time and therefore inaccessible to most people. But as sugar prices dropped over the years, more couples could feature a white frosted cake at their wedding.

In the early 1900s, another frosting made of egg whites and sugar rose to popularity. It was known as "boiled" frosting because its sugar was boiled into a hot syrup before being beaten into egg whites. Buttercream is another frosting that dates to the early 1900s. As its name suggests, the frosting has a butter base that lends a richer taste than egg white frostings.

By the mid-1900s, consumers could purchase ready-made frosting in cans and jars. To this day, popular baking brands like Betty Crocker and Pillsbury sell canned frostings and icings alongside boxed cake and cookie mixes. These products have the look of a buttercream or boiled frosting but are made of mostly sugar and oil. They appeal to consumers who want a home-baked dessert but are short on time or ingredients.

While store-bought frostings and icings are convenient, many bakers argue that the taste and quality of homemade frostings and icings cannot be beat. In the following pages, you'll learn about common ingredients, tools, and techniques used to make a variety of frostings and icings from scratch. Then you'll be ready to decorate all your favorite desserts!

Many grocery stores sell canned frostings to accompany baking mixes. Customers can choose from a variety of flavors.

INGREDIENTS

Get familiar with some of the ingredients you'll see in this book's recipes.

ALMOND EXTRACT

Almond extract is made with the oil of bitter almonds. It is often used to flavor different frostings and icings, such as the royal icing in this book. Almond extract has a very strong flavor, so start with a quarter teaspoon and taste before adding more.

BUTTER

Butter is a fat typically made from cow's milk. It provides the soft, creamy structure and rich flavor in buttercream frosting. Butter is also sometimes used in ganache, to which it adds richness and shine. Use unsalted butter in frostings and icings so you can control how much salt is added.

CREAM OF TARTAR

Cream of tartar is a white acidic powder that's commonly used to help stabilize whipped egg whites so they don't deflate. Cream of tartar also helps prevent sugar crystals from forming when boiling sugar into syrup.

EGG WHITES

Egg whites provide structure in frostings and icings. This is because egg whites contain proteins that unravel when the eggs are whipped. The proteins then reform around the pockets of air whipped into the eggs. Egg whites must be heated to 160°F to be considered safe for consumption. That's why many royal icing recipes recommend using pasteurized liquid egg whites instead of raw eggs.

GEL-BASED FOOD COLORING

Gel-based food coloring is made with corn syrup or glycerin. This gives the product a more viscous consistency than liquid food coloring, which has a water base. Gel-based coloring is recommended for frostings and icings because it won't thin them out and the colors are more vibrant.

GRANULATED SUGAR

Sugar adds sweetness to frostings and icings. Recipes that call for "white sugar" or simply "sugar" are referring to granulated sugar. It is made of sugar cane or sugar beets that have been juiced, boiled, and refined into white granules. Meringue frostings use granulated sugar that is cooked with egg whites.

HEAVY CREAM

Heavy cream, also called heavy whipping cream, is the thick part of fresh milk that rises to the top due to its high fat content. When heavy cream is whipped, pockets of air get trapped in the network of fat droplets, turning the cream into a light and airy fluff. Whipped cream is used as the base of many frostings. In this book, ganache is an emulsion of heavy cream and chocolate. Heavy cream is also used in the buttercream recipe to create a silky, creamy texture.

LEMON JUICE

Lemon juice is added to some icings to balance out their sweetness. In royal icing, its acidity also helps stabilize the whipped egg whites.

LIGHT CORN SYRUP

Corn syrup is a thick, sweet syrup made from the natural sugars in corn. It is often used to add moisture and shine to frostings. Light corn syrup has a mildly sweet flavor. Dark corn syrup has a deeper, richer flavor due to added molasses.

POWDERED SUGAR

Powdered sugar, also known as confectioner's sugar or icing sugar, is granulated sugar that has been pulverized into a fine powder. It often contains added cornstarch, which prevents the sugar from clumping. Powdered sugar dissolves at room temperature, making it preferred over granulated sugar for buttercream, royal icing, and other uncooked frostings and icings.

SEMISWEET CHOCOLATE

Semisweet chocolate has about 40 to 60 percent cocoa. This produces a nice balance of sweetness and bitterness. The ganache in this book calls for semisweet chocolate, but you can also make ganaches out of white, milk, or dark chocolates. Darker ganaches are more bitter and best paired with sweet desserts. Conversely, lighter ganaches are sweeter and best paired with bitter, tart, or salty flavors.

VANILLA EXTRACT

Vanilla extract adds a subtle flavor to frostings and icings. Pure vanilla extract is made by soaking vanilla beans in an alcohol solution. This pulls out the flavors of the vanilla beans and concentrates them in liquid form. If you want your frosting or icing to be as white as possible, use clear vanilla, an imitation extract made with artificial vanilla flavor.

KITCHEN TOOLS

Get familiar with some of the supplies you'll see in this book's recipes.

BLENDER

A blender is an electrical kitchen appliance that uses a motorized blade to mix, puree, or liquefy ingredients. You can use a blender to puree fruits into juice to flavor frostings and icings.

ELECTRIC MIXER

Both stand mixers and handheld mixers use electricity to whip ingredients, such as butter or egg whites, for frostings and icings. It is possible to make buttercream, royal icing, and other sweet spreads without an electric mixer—it just takes a little more time and muscle!

BROILER

The broiler is the part of an oven that exposes dishes to high heat for quick browning. It is usually located on the ceiling of the oven, but in some ovens the broiler is in a drawer at the bottom of the appliance. In this book, a broiler is used to caramelize the sugar at the surface of meringue frosting for a toasted-marshmallow effect. This can also be done with a kitchen torch, a handheld tool that produces a flame for quick caramelization.

HEATPROOF MIXING BOWL

A heatproof bowl is one that can withstand heat without burning, melting, or warping. Frostings and icings that use heat, such as ganache and meringue frosting, require such a bowl. Glass, stainless steel, and ceramic are all heatproof materials.

OFFSET SPATULA

An offset spatula is a long and flexible metal blade with a handle at one end and a rounded edge at the other. The blade of the spatula bends downward off the handle, creating more space between your hand and the frosting you are spreading. This gives you better control as you spread frosting or icing on your desserts. If you don't have an offset spatula, use a regular spatula, butter knife, or spoon.

PASTRY BAGS & TIPS

A pastry bag or piping bag is a cone-shaped bag that holds frostings and icings that must be piped. The bag is filled through its large opening. The filling is then squeezed out of the small opening, which is often fitted with a metal tip that helps shape the piped filling. If you do not have a pastry bag and tip, scoop your frosting or icing into a plastic bag and cut an opening in one of the bag's bottom corners.

SAUCEPAN

A saucepan is a piece of cookware with a flat circular base; tall, straight sides; and one long handle. It is meant for cooking liquids on the stove. In this book, you need a saucepan to heat up cream for ganache. You will also use a saucepan to create a double boiler for whipping up a meringue frosting.

SIEVE

A sieve is a bowl-shaped utensil with a long handle. The bowl is made of wire mesh that separates solids from liquids or breaks up any lumps in dry ingredients. As described on page 34, you can use a sieve to remove the seeds from blended raspberries to get a smooth puree. Bakers also use sieves to sift powdered sugar to remove any clumps.

THERMOMETER

Some meringue frostings call for cooking egg whites and sugar to 160°F. A candy thermometer reads up to about 400°F and can clip to the side of a saucepan. You can also use a meat thermometer, which reads up to about 200°F but does not typically come with a clip.

WHISK

A whisk is used to blend ingredients quickly and thoroughly. In this book, it is used to blend sugar and egg whites over heat for the meringue frosting. It is also used to emulsify cream and chocolate for the ganache. Thicker frostings, such as buttercreams, will clog up inside whisks and therefore require stronger mixing tools, such as rubber spatulas.

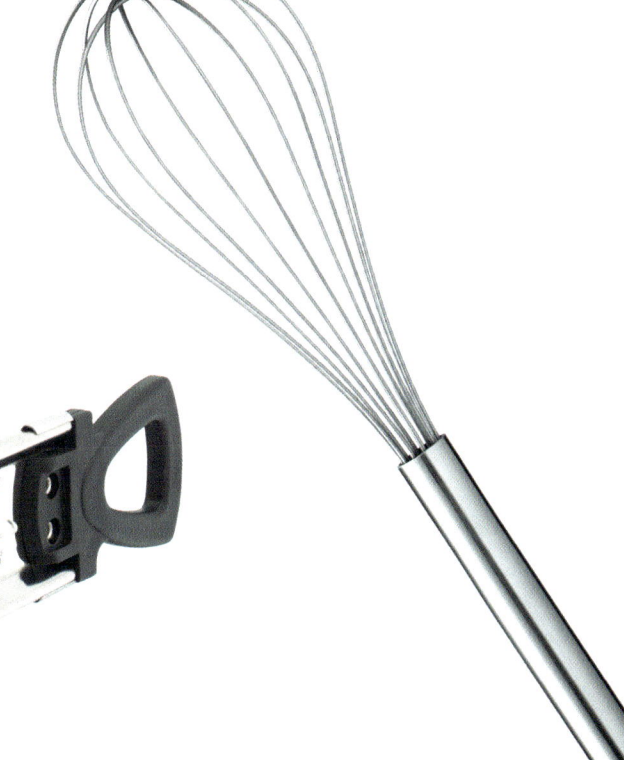

TERMS & TECHNIQUES

Get familiar with some of the terms and techniques you'll see in this book's recipes.

DOUBLE BOILER

A double boiler is a cooking device made of two pots: a large one that is filled with water and set on the stove, and a smaller one that rests on top of the large pot. As the water in the bottom pot simmers, it gently heats the ingredients in the top pot. This method is commonly used to heat chocolate, eggs, and other ingredients that do not hold up well to direct heat. Many bakers create makeshift double boilers using a regular saucepan and a heatproof bowl. Just make sure the bowl can rest on the rim of the saucepan without touching the simmering water in the pan.

FLOODING

Flooding refers to covering a cookie with thinned royal icing to create a smooth, hard surface for decorating. Before flooding, outline the cookie with regular royal icing. This creates a dam that prevents the flooded icing from spilling over the cookie's edge.

SEPARATING EGG WHITES FROM YOLKS

An egg consists of the yellow yolk and the white. Some frosting and icing recipes call for just egg whites, which contain proteins that provide structure. To separate the white from the yolk, crack the egg over a bowl. Gently pass the yolk back and forth between the shell halves until all of the white has slipped off the yolk and into the bowl. Then place the yolk into a different container. Save the yolks to make custard, pasta, ice cream, and more!

PIPING

Piping frosting or icing means squeezing the mixture from a bag onto a surface. Sometimes special tips are used to create distinct shapes. Piping techniques vary depending on the mixture you are piping, the tip you are using, and the shape you are making. Pipe a few practice shapes on a plate or piece of parchment to get a feel for the pressure and angle to pipe at.

SIMMERING VERSUS BOILING

If a recipe says to heat a liquid to a simmer, look for small bubbles that rise to the liquid's surface, causing gentle movement. If a recipe calls for boiling the liquid, look for many large bubbles rising at once, constantly disrupting the liquid's surface.

SOFT VERSUS STIFF PEAKS

The terms *soft peaks* and *stiff peaks* are used to describe the strength of a whipped substance, such as egg whites or cream. To test this, turn over your whisk or mixer attachments and observe how the egg whites react. If they form a peak that curls down with gravity, they have reached "soft peaks." If they form a peak that stays firmly upright, they have reached "stiff peaks."

SOFTENING BUTTER

Most buttercream recipes call for softened butter. Take your butter out of the refrigerator a couple hours before you make your buttercream so it can come to room temperature. This makes it easier to whip the butter to a fluffy consistency and incorporate the sugar. If you need to soften butter in a hurry, cut it into smaller pieces and place it near a warm oven. But don't let the butter get too soft or start to melt. This will result in a thin, greasy buttercream.

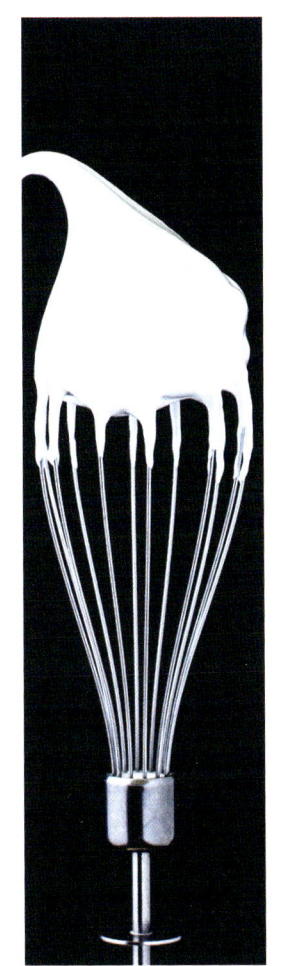
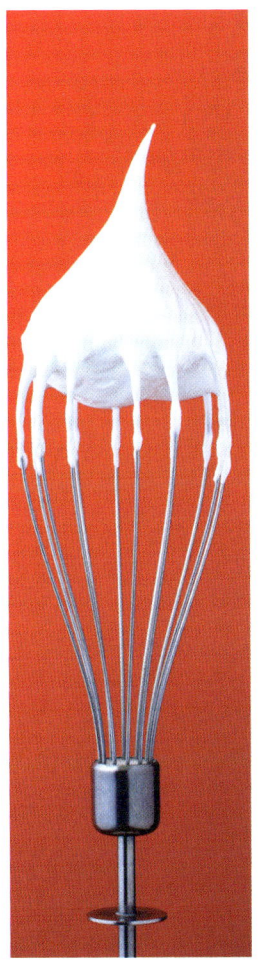

KITCHEN PREP TIPS

> Have all your supplies out and ready before you begin. Gather all your ingredients on a tray or rimmed baking sheet. Then it's easy to slide everything out of the way if you need to make space.

> Wear an apron to protect your clothing. It will also serve as a hand towel.

FROSTING & ICING TIPS & TRICKS

Bakers can encounter a number of issues when whipping up frostings and icings. Here are a few tips and tricks to set yourself up for success.

BUTTERCREAM

- Remember, recipes call for softened butter for a reason. Avoid using cold butter in your buttercream, as this can result in a curdled texture.

- Add enough liquid to make your buttercream creamy, but not so much that it's thin and soupy.

- Avoid overwhipping the buttercream. This will create air bubbles in the frosting as you spread or pipe it.

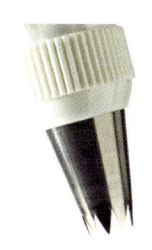

MERINGUE FROSTING

- It is easier to separate whites from yolks when eggs are cold. Do this right after you take the eggs out of the refrigerator. Then let the whites come to room temperature, which makes them easier to whip.

- Whip egg whites in a clean, dry bowl with a clean, dry whisk. Any bit of grease or fat will prevent the whites from whipping properly.

- Meringue frosting becomes stiff with time, so do any spreading or piping soon after the frosting is prepared.

GANACHE

- Even a small bit of water will cause ganache to seize up, or clump. Make sure the bowl you use to make the ganache is fully dry. Once the ganache is made, avoid covering it until it has fully cooled. This will prevent droplets of condensation from ruining the ganache.

- Let the cream come to a simmer but not a boil. If the cream is too hot, it will cause the fat in the chocolate to separate, giving your ganache a grainy texture.

- Overstirring can also result in a grainy ganache. Stop stirring the ganache as soon as the chocolate and cream become smooth and silky.

ROYAL ICING

- Sifting the powdered sugar through a sieve helps prevent small clumps of sugar in your royal icing.

- Once you've flooded a cookie with royal icing, tap it on the table to bring any air bubbles to the surface. Then use a toothpick to pop the air bubbles. Do this right after flooding the cookie, as the icing will harden quickly.

- Instead of dragging the piping tip along the surface of the cookie, keep the tip slightly above the surface so the icing falls onto the cookie. This results in straighter piping lines.

FOOD SAFETY TIPS

> Make sure your prep surface is clean and dry. Wash your hands with soap and water before and after you handle ingredients.

> Don't eat uncooked eggs. Thoroughly wash your hands after cracking eggs.

> Place any leftover ingredients into containers with lids. Use tape and markers to label the container with the ingredient and the date. Then keep it somewhere you will easily see it so you don't forget about it.

CREATING IN THE KITCHEN

Recipes are great for learning how to make frosting and icing. But as you get comfortable following recipes, you might start imagining ways to improve them.

Maybe you want to add some salt and caramel to your ganache. Or maybe you decide to thin out your buttercream with orange juice instead of heavy cream.

This book includes four formal recipes meant to help you practice working with different ingredients and techniques. Following each formal recipe is an informal companion. These companion recipes are less structured and provide fewer details. This leaves room for you, the baker, to follow your own tastes and preferences. If an informal recipe doesn't suit your taste, check out the accompanying "Experiment!" sidebar for additional ideas. With some thought and creativity, you can make any recipe your own way.

CONVERSION CHART

Standard	Metric
¼ teaspoon	1.25 mL
½ teaspoon	2.5 mL
1 teaspoon	5 mL
1 tablespoon	15 mL
¼ cup	60 mL
⅓ cup	80 mL
½ cup	125 mL
⅔ cup	160 mL
¾ cup	175 mL
1 cup	240 mL
160°F	71°C
325°F	160°C
350°F	180°C
375°F	190°C
400°F	200°C

RULES TO REMEMBER

As you start putting your own twist on recipes, keep these guiding principles in mind.

Master the basics first. Start out following recipes exactly as they are written. You'll better understand how ingredients combine and behave, and this knowledge will inform your decisions as you go off-book.

Every baker has their own methods. You might see another baker whip up their meringue frosting differently than you do. Or, another baker may use different supplies to pipe their royal icing. This doesn't mean you have to change your ingredients or techniques. If you can, ask a baker why their methods work for them. Test the methods yourself and decide what works best for you!

Experiments don't always go to plan. Don't be crushed if your buttercream is runny or your ganache is grainy. Most frostings and icings can be fixed! For example, runny buttercream can be chilled in the refrigerator and re-whipped, and grainy ganache can be gently reheated over a saucepan of simmering water. Even if you don't nail the texture you want, your creation is probably still edible. Turn it into a sweet dip for cookies, graham crackers, or strawberries!

Baking is often called a precise science. But a recipe won't be ruined by an extra tablespoon of powdered sugar or a missed teaspoon of vanilla. Bakers are always tweaking and testing their recipes. Enjoy the process and take pride in the results.

BUTTERCREAM FROSTING

Buttercream is made with a base of fat—usually butter—and sugar. The result is a soft, buttery frosting, making it popular for decorating a wide variety of baked goods.

INGREDIENTS

> 1 cup unsalted butter, softened
> 4 cups powdered sugar
> 2 teaspoons vanilla extract
> 3-5 tablespoons heavy cream

SUPPLIES

> large mixing bowl
> electric mixer
> measuring cup and spoons
> spoon, offset spatula, spreading knife, or pastry bag(s) with tip(s)

1

Place the butter in the mixing bowl. Then, using an electric mixer, whip the butter on medium-high speed until it is smooth and creamy.

2

Turn the mixer to low speed and add the powdered sugar about 1 cup at a time. Make sure each cup of sugar is incorporated before adding the next.

3

Add the vanilla extract and heavy cream to the bowl.

4

Beat the mixture on low speed until everything is combined. Then turn the mixer up to high speed and whip the frosting for a few more minutes.

5 If you'd like your buttercream to be thinner, beat in more cream, about 1 teaspoon at a time. If you'd like it to be thicker, beat in more powdered sugar, about 1 tablespoon at a time.

6

Spread or pipe your buttercream over fully cooled baked goods.

BERRY
BUTTERCREAM

Brighten up a basic buttercream with a tart raspberry puree!

Puree raspberries in a blender. Pour the blended berries through a sieve to remove the seeds. Use a spatula to push as much puree as possible through the sieve.

EXPERIMENT!

Grind freeze-dried fruit into a powder and use that to flavor and color your buttercream. Replace some of the butter with cream cheese for a slightly tart frosting. Make a chocolate buttercream by adding cocoa powder or cooled melted chocolate to the base.

Prepare a basic buttercream, but before adding cream, gradually whip in the raspberry puree. Add cream after to thin out the frosting if desired.

Pipe the raspberry buttercream onto cakes or other baked goods.

MERINGUE FROSTING

This light and airy frosting is made by whipping sugar and egg whites over a double boiler. This creates a marshmallow-like spread!

INGREDIENTS

- > water
- > 2 egg whites, room temperature
- > ⅓ cup granulated sugar
- > ⅓ cup light corn syrup
- > ¼ teaspoon cream of tartar
- > 1 teaspoon vanilla extract

SUPPLIES

- > saucepan
- > stove
- > heatproof mixing bowl
- > measuring cups and spoons
- > whisk
- > thermometer
- > electric mixer
- > spoon, offset spatula, spreading knife, or pastry bag(s) with tip(s)

1

Fill the saucepan with about ½ inch (1.3 cm) of water. Heat the pan on the stove until the water comes to a simmer.

2

In the bowl, combine the egg whites, sugar, corn syrup, and cream of tartar.

3

Place the bowl over the pan of simmering water so the bowl rests on the rim of the pan. The water should not touch the bottom of the bowl.

4

Whisk everything together over the simmering water until the mixture's temperature reaches 160°F.

5

Remove from heat and continue whipping the frosting with the electric mixer until it has cooled slightly.

6

Add the vanilla extract to the frosting. Then keep whipping it until soft peaks form.

7

Spread or pipe the meringue frosting onto your dessert.

TOASTED MARSHMALLOW
FROSTING

Pipe your meringue frosting into fluffy clouds and apply heat for a toasted-marshmallow effect!

Mix up a batch of meringue frosting.

EXPERIMENT!

Try substituting brown sugar for white sugar for a deeper flavor. Flavor your frosting with citrus zest instead of vanilla extract. Or chill your frosted cupcakes in the freezer before dipping the fluffy clouds of frosting into melted chocolate!

Fill a pastry bag and pipe swirls of the frosting over cupcakes.

Place the cupcakes under your oven's broiler so they are a few inches from the heating element. Watch for the frosting to turn a toasty golden brown!

GANACHE ICING

Ganache is a mix of chocolate and heavy cream. You can adjust the ratio of these ingredients depending on how thick or thin you want your ganache to be. Some bakers also add butter for richness and extracts for flavor.

INGREDIENTS

- 10 ounces (283.5 g) chopped semisweet chocolate (or 1½ cups chocolate chips)
- 1 cup heavy cream
- 2 tablespoons unsalted butter
- 1 teaspoon vanilla extract

SUPPLIES

- measuring cups and spoons
- heatproof mixing bowl
- small saucepan
- stove
- whisk
- knife and cutting board

1 Pour the chocolate into the mixing bowl.

2

Heat the heavy cream in the saucepan over low heat until it starts to simmer.

3

Pour the hot cream over the chocolate. Let it sit for about a minute while the chocolate melts.

4

Whisk the cream and chocolate together until the mixture is smooth and all the chocolate has melted.

5

Cut the butter into ½-inch (1.3 cm) cubes. Add them to the chocolate along with the vanilla extract.

6

Continue stirring the mixture until all the butter is melted and incorporated.

7

Pour or drizzle the ganache over baked goods. You can also dip small treats, such as doughnuts, into the ganache.

GANACHE FROSTING

Turn your ganache icing into fluffy whipped frosting that's perfect for piping!

Make ganache and let it cool in the refrigerator until it becomes stiff.

EXPERIMENT!

Try using different ingredients to flavor your ganache, such as orange zest, peppermint extract, or espresso powder. If your ganache is thinner than you'd like, add some more chocolate. If it is too thick, add some more hot cream or heat it in the microwave in 10-second intervals.

Use an electric mixer to whip the ganache until it is light and fluffy.

Fill a pastry bag with the whipped ganache and pipe the frosting onto your dessert.

ROYAL ICING

Royal icing is a mix of egg whites and powdered sugar. This thick, smooth icing dries hard, making it perfect for piping decorative details on cakes and cookies.

INGREDIENTS

- ½ cup pasteurized liquid egg whites (or 3 large pasteurized egg whites)
- 4 cups powdered sugar
- 1 teaspoon lemon juice
- ½ teaspoon almond extract
- gel-based food coloring (optional)

SUPPLIES

- measuring cups and spoons
- mixing bowl
- electric mixer
- rubber spatula
- spoons
- pastry bag(s) with tip(s)

1

Place the egg whites in the mixing bowl. With an electric mixer, beat the egg whites at medium-high speed until they are frothy.

2

Turn the mixer to low speed. Gradually incorporate the powdered sugar. Use a rubber spatula to carefully scrape down the sides of the bowl as you go.

3

Once all the powdered sugar is fully incorporated, add the lemon juice and almond extract.

4

Beat the mixture on high speed for a few minutes. The mixture should be thick and shiny.

5

Mix your choice of food coloring into the icing. If you want to create multiple colors, divide the icing into separate bowls before adding colors.

6

Transfer the icing to one or more pastry bags and start decorating!

FLOOD ICING

Thin out your royal icing to cover, or "flood," sugar cookies with a perfectly smooth layer of icing.

Choose a base color for your cookies. Use this color to outline the cookies.

EXPERIMENT!

Try different extracts to flavor your royal icing, such as vanilla or peppermint. If your icing feels too thick, add a little bit of water. If it feels too thin, add a little more powdered sugar. Use sugar pearls or other fun sprinkles to enhance your icing decorations!

Mix a little bit of water into the outline color. This thins out the icing so you can flood the cookie with it.

Once the flooded icing is set, pipe on details with other colors.

PRESENTATION & BEYOND

Your frostings and icings are whipped and ready, but you're not done yet! It's time to think about how you want to show off your creation. Just as important is how you preserve any leftovers.

Use an offset spatula to smooth out buttercream or create swirls of texture. You can also pipe buttercream using tips of all shapes and sizes.

Show off the cloudlike texture of meringue frosting by spreading swirls of it over cakes or piping tall towers of it over cupcakes.

Dip cookies in ganache and leave its smooth, shiny surface undisturbed. Or, pour ganache over cakes and let it drip down the sides.

Royal icing is perfect for piping intricate details on baked goods. You can also use it to create a smooth icing canvas for edible paint!

STORING FROSTINGS & ICINGS

Store unused frostings and icings in airtight containers. For best results, place plastic wrap directly on top of the frosting to prevent it from drying out. Use the table below as a rough guide for where and how long you can store the frostings and icings in this book.

Icing	Room Temperature	Refrigerator	Freezer
BUTTERCREAM	Two days	Seven days	Three months
MERINGUE	One day	Two days	Not recommended
GANACHE	A few hours	Two weeks	Three months
ROYAL ICING	Not recommended*	Three days	One month

*Royal icing made with meringue powder instead of egg whites can be stored at room temperature for up to two weeks.

BECOMING A DESSERT DECORATOR

As you gain more knowledge and experience making frostings and icings, you might decide to turn your hobby into a living. There are many ways to pursue a career in dessert decoration!

FORMAL SCHOOLING

Culinary and technical schools offer baking and pastry programs that last anywhere from a few months to several years. These programs offer instruction in making pastries, decorating cakes, and more. They also prepare students for work in professional kitchens.

COMMUNITY CLASSES

Many local businesses, such as craft stores and kitchen supply stores, offer classes in cake decoration. You can also look for classes through community education programs in your city.

APPRENTICESHIP

Professional kitchens offer hands-on experience through apprenticeships and internships. These positions are often part-time and unpaid.

ON-THE-JOB TRAINING

Some establishments hire employees with no formal training. New bakers and pastry artists learn from experienced coworkers.

SELF-TEACHING

Many professional bakers and pastry chefs learned what they know by reading cookbooks, watching videos, and practicing in their own kitchens.

DESSERT PROS AT WORK

As a dessert decorator, you can work in a variety of establishments. Read about a few of them below. Think about which suit you best and why.

RETAIL BAKERIES

Retail bakeries produce, package, and sell baked goods directly to customers. Some specialize in highly stylized cakes and cupcakes for weddings and other special occasions.

WHOLESALE BAKERIES

Wholesale bakeries are high-volume operations that produce baked goods to be sold in bulk to restaurants, grocery stores, and other establishments.

RESTAURANTS

Some restaurants employ full- or part-time bakers or pastry artists to make and decorate baked goods for diners.

GROCERY STORE BAKERIES

Many grocery stores hire bakers or pastry artists to produce freshly baked goods. These goods are then sold at the store.

HOME OR RENTED BAKERY

Some bakers and pastry artists operate out of their home kitchens and sell goods to small shops or at farmers markets. Be sure to know your local laws before starting a business from your home. Alternatively, many professionals rent commercial kitchen spaces.

Depending on where you work, baking professionally can be drastically different from home baking. As you think about baking for a living, consider some of the tools, rules, and schedules of a professional baker.

TOOLS

The tools of a professional decorator are built to produce large quantities of frostings, icings, and baked goods. Commercial ovens and cooling racks hold dozens of baked goods at a time. Industrial mixers whip up gallons of frosting in minutes. Commercial kitchens also order bulk ingredients, such as 25-pound (11.3 kg) bags of powdered sugar. Workers must be able to safely lift these heavy supplies.

RULES

Bakers and pastry artists must uphold cleanliness and food safety standards. These standards range from wearing a uniform and keeping hair pulled back to properly storing ingredients and thoroughly cleaning equipment after use. Workers must also follow rules to protect themselves and others from kitchen hazards, such as hot pans and wet floors.

SCHEDULES

Many bakers start their work early in the morning. This way, their baked goods can be cooled, frosted, and ready to sell a few hours later. Dessert decorators must be able to stay on their feet and maintain close attention to detail for many hours at a time. Retail bakeries and restaurants are especially busy during weekends, so most bakers and pastry artists work at least one weekend day.

DO WHAT YOU LOVE!

Being a dessert decorator requires long shifts, hard physical work, and attention to rules and standards. These requirements can be difficult for home bakers to adjust to. But many professionals find the rewards of their work outweigh the difficulties. These rewards include being creative, getting exercise, and learning new skills.

Maybe your goal is to sell iced cookies at local markets. Maybe you have your sights set on opening a cupcake shop. Or perhaps you are happy to keep baking as a hobby but not as a career. As long as you do what you love, you'll love what you do.

GLOSSARY

appliance—a household or office device operated by gas or electric power. Common kitchen appliances include stoves, refrigerators, and dishwashers.

apprenticeship—an arrangement in which a person learns a trade or a craft from a skilled worker.

caramelize—to cook a food until the sugars in it brown, creating a sweet, nutty flavor. This process is called caramelization.

culinary—having to do with the kitchen or cooking.

edible—safe to eat.

embellish—to make something more attractive by adding details.

emulsify—to combine liquids that don't dissolve into each other so that the liquids are spread out throughout each other in a mixture. An emulsion is an emulsified mixture.

enhance—to increase or make better.

establishment—a place or organization where people do business.

glycerin—a thick, sweet liquid that is removed from fats and oils.

granule—a small, firm particle of a substance. A granulated substance is made of many small particles.

incorporate—to include or work into.

industrial—of or having to do with factories and making things in large quantities.

internship—a program that allows a student or graduate to gain guided practical experience in a professional field.

molasses—the thick, brown syrup obtained as sugarcane is processed into sugar.

multitiered–made up of more than one level.

pasteurized–having been heated for a certain amount of time in order to destroy bacteria and other harmful organisms without otherwise changing the substance.

pulverize–to crush or grind into very fine particles.

retail–related to the selling of goods directly to customers. Businesses that sell goods directly to customers are called retailers.

technique–a method or style in which something is done.

unravel–to cause the separate threads of something to come apart.

viscous–thick and sticky in consistency.

wholesale–relating to businesses that sell things in large amounts, often directly to other businesses.

ONLINE RESOURCES

To learn more about careers as a dessert decorator, please visit **abdobooklinks.com** or scan this QR code. These links are routinely monitored and updated to provide the most current information available.

INDEX